New York's Capital District

1978–2003

Tom Killips

ARCADIA

Copyright © Tom Killips
ISBN 0-7385-3495-1

First published 2004

Published by Arcadia Publishing,
an imprint of Tempus Publishing Inc.
Portsmouth NH, Charleston SC,
Chicago, San Francisco

Printed in Great Britain

Library of Congress Catalog Card Number: 2003116041

For all general information, contact Arcadia Publishing:
Telephone 843-853-2070
Fax 843-853-0044
E-mail sales@arcadiapublishing.com
For customer service and orders:
Toll-free 1-888-313-2665

Visit us on the Internet at www.arcadiapublishing.com

*Dedicated to my wife, Deborah,
and children, Rachel and Brian.*

A REFLECTED FIREMAN. Bob Durivage, a past chief of the DeFreestville Fire Department, adjusts the flag attached to the mirror of the fire engine he drove in the Rensselaer Memorial Day parade. (5/28/2000)

New York's Capital District

1978–2003

CUOMO REFLECTS. Gov. Mario Cuomo strikes a reflective pose after meeting with reporters in his office on a Saturday morning. The legislature wrapped up its session that morning, and Cuomo expressed frustration with the lack of progress in several areas. (7/1/1989)

Contents

Acknowledgments   6

Introduction   7

1.   News   9

2.   Features   47

3.   Sports   75

4.   Arts and Entertainment   105

ACKNOWLEDGEMENTS

This book would not have been possible without the support and cooperation of my employer for the past 25 years, the Record newspapers in Troy. Editor Lisa Robert Lewis, in particular, has been of enormous assistance.

Features editor Doug de Lisle, sports editor Kevin Moran, chief photographer Mike McMahon, and my colleagues in the photography department, Jim Carras, Jeff Couch, and Susan B. Cummings, have all assisted and supported my efforts in assembling this extensive collection of photographs.

Kevin Gilbert, another Record colleague, was invaluable in helping to research the photographs to provide complete and accurate captions.

Neil McGreevy and his exceptional staff at McGreevy Pro Lab in Albany are responsible for helping to ensure each photograph was scanned for the best possible reproduction.

Last, but certainly not least, is the support, advice, and cooperation of my wife, Deborah LaClair Killips. A graphic artist, designer, and art teacher, she always offers valued guidance and input.

AN ROTC PORTRAIT. Tracy Ridley (left) and John Scott, ROTC members from Rensselaer Polytechnic Institute in Troy, go through field training exercises in Grafton Lakes State Park. The simulated combat conditions were designed to prepare seniors for summer camp at Fort Bragg, North Carolina. (10/12/1985)

INTRODUCTION

For the past 25 years, it has been my job to photograph the news and newsmakers of the Capital District. In that role, I have taken almost 450,000 images—187 of which are featured in this book.

The editing process proved difficult. With an overwhelming number of choices available, some people and stories were inevitably left out. While I now shoot all of my work in color, at least half the images in this book were originally done in black and white, and a decision was made early in the production process to reproduce the images in black and white, thereby avoiding the distraction color can have on a photograph's message.

I hope the collection I ultimately selected will prove interesting to a wide range of people, whether they be lifelong Capital District residents or people new to this region.

While working each day, my goal is to make the strongest storytelling photographs possible that represent the story fairly and accurately. As a daily newspaper photojournalist, I do not think in historical terms while working. It was not until I reviewed some of my older images that I realized how many people and places are not around anymore.

It is never my goal to make anyone look bad—or good, for that matter. My goal is to find the most interesting picture.

I have never taken pleasure in witnessing another person's pain, although I accept that my job sometimes requires coverage of news events where this is inevitable. The photograph of a mother's anguish as she learns her daughter died in a fire (page 11) is this type of image. At such times, I am thankful for long lenses so I can maintain a respectful distance.

The most challenging assignments are the "enterprise," or feature, photographs. These unplanned photographs, usually of people doing something interesting or unusual, are in constant need at most daily newspapers. The images of children doing backflips off a mattress (page 72) and the golfing nun (page 74) are examples of this type of picture.

Unlike globetrotting photojournalists who travel the world in pursuit of the big story, community newspaper photographers typically do their work within a 25-mile radius of the office. Trying to find new images regularly in your own backyard is a challenge. In fact, some photographers define a good day by the number of U-turns they make while driving around seeking photographs.

Most daily newspaper photographers, myself included, are the quintessential general assignment photographers. You are as likely to cover a major news story as a sporting event or a studio shot, sometimes all in the same day. The ability to think quickly on your feet and handle a variety of assignments is essential for a working news photographer.

In my quest to find unusual angles, I occasionally use remote setups so I can cover major events with multiple cameras. When using a remote, I prefocus one camera on a zone with everything set so a switch on a remote cord can trigger the shot. At the same time, I can be using another camera, capturing yet another view of the same event. My wife, Deborah, and her brothers, John and Matt LaClair, are the people I rely on most to push the trigger on my remotes. The photograph of Point Given winning the Travers at the Saratoga Race Course (page 95) was done remotely.

Another point of view I find interesting is the high angle that can be achieved with an aerial photograph. The photographs of the train derailment (page 13) and the wing walker (page 68), which was also done with a remote, are examples of how an aerial view can help show the enormity of a situation on the ground.

Some of the most memorable moments I have shot during the past 25 years were sporting events. When New York Yankees ace Ron Guidry pitched at Heritage Park (page 90), the crowd overflowed the Colonie stadium. The fans were even allowed to sit on the field against the outfield fence for the special occasion.

Mike Tyson's early fights (page 80) were incredible, and the crowds were always at fever pitch since Tyson usually knocked out his opponent quickly.

Michael Jordan's appearance with the Chicago Bulls at a preseason game against the Knicks (page 96) was another high point. Traffic backed up on the Northway as the crowd headed to a packed Glens Falls Civic Center. Jordan did not disappoint; it was obvious he was going to be special kind of player.

Without question my favorite subjects are people. I am still amazed at what some people are able to do. While I get to observe people at work and at play, it is the real characters that typically make the most interesting subjects.

One of my favorite characters is Prof. Bill Steed (page 58), the dean of Croaker College. He brought with him a collection of bullfrogs dressed in children's costumes who performed tricks using children's toys.

These are only a few of the moments captured in this book. I have photographed all types—famous people and lesser-known ones, many of whom are featured in this intriguing collection.

I hope you enjoy my look back at the past 25 years as much as I have enjoyed covering them.

SKATERS. People skate on the frozen reflecting pond at the Empire State Plaza late in the afternoon with the state capitol in the background. Every winter, this area continues to be a popular place for skating. (12/29/1978)

A TREED BEAR. Officers from the New York State Department of Environmental Conservation hold a net as the bear makes one last climb up the tree before giving up. The black bear was spotted on the Emma Willard campus in Troy and spent most of the day high in an oak tree. It finally came down but never went to sleep despite three tranquilizer darts. The bear, which was tagged, was returned to the neighboring state of Massachusetts, where it belonged. (5/24/1985)

THE MANCINI FIRE. Flames from the second-floor apartments lick the sides of the Mancini Travel Agency building in downtown Troy. The fire destroyed the building and occurred within hours of the South End Van Lines fire. (2/16/1979)

THE SOUTH END VAN LINES FIRE. Troy firefighters pour water on a warehouse that housed South End Van Lines. Two warehouses were destroyed in the stubborn fire. (2/16/1979)

IN ANGUISH. Rose Davis, held by Troy police officer Thomas Kane, screams in anguish after learning her daughter died in a fire at Corliss Park Apartments in Troy. The tragic fire began in the kitchen, and Mary Ellen Davis, 36, was overcome by smoke and died near that room. (2/2/1983)

THE TROY CLUB FIRE. Flames turn the Troy Club, built in 1887, into a raging inferno. The fire, fanned by strong winds, burned through the night and destroyed the building, located at Congress and First Streets in Troy. (3/26/1981)

THE FIRE'S AFTERMATH. Troy firefighters wet down the charred remains of the Troy Club, which was destroyed in a spectacular fire. Firefighters believed the fire started in the rear of the second floor above the kitchen. (3/27/1981)

A TANKER FIRE. Firefighters use foam to extinguish a fire after a gas tanker collided with another car in Buskirk. The tanker contained 8,500 gallons of gasoline. Amazingly no one was seriously injured in the accident, to which seven fire companies responded. (11/4/1981)

A TRAIN DERAILMENT. Scattered along the tracks are some of the 33 cars of a Boston & Maine freight train that derailed in the village of Eagle Bridge. The primary concern was the three propane tankers in the middle, which fortunately held together. (2/3/1980)

THE THRUWAY COLLAPSE. Tragedy struck on April 5, 1987, in Fort Hunter when 326 feet of the New York State Thruway spanning the Schoharie Creek collapsed, killing 10 people. Raging waters from heavy rain caused the creek to swell and undermine the middle pier, plunging five cars 75 feet into the water. The recovery effort was lengthy, and one body was not located until nearly a year later in the Hudson River miles from the scene. (4/8/1987)

A THRUWAY FATALITY. A Wisconsin couple was killed when their car was crushed by a tractor trailer that later burst into flames near exit 23 of the New York State Thruway. The tragic accident shut down the road for hours. (8/24/1988)

DIGGING OUT. People on Second Street in Troy dig out from the blizzard, which began during the St. Patrick's Day parade. More than two feet of snow fell, shutting roads and making travel impossible. (3/14/1993)

SKIING THE APPROACH. Rensselaer Polytechnic Institute seniors Bill Benner (left) and Brian Thomm ski off the Approach after a blizzard buried the stone steps in snow. The Approach, which connects downtown Troy to the campus on the hill, was in disrepair for many years before it was restored. (3/14/1993)

THE MATTY SHER FIRE. Firefighters throw water on a stubborn fire at Matty Sher's Auto Parts in East Greenbush. Five fire companies fought the blaze, which destroyed the store. (12/3/1982)

THE FIRE AT DELSON'S. Firefighters pour water onto the burning Delson's Supermarket in Nassau. Members of 31 surrounding companies battled three fires in the small Rensselaer County village that same afternoon. Delson's, a local landmark, was destroyed. The fires caused more than $1 million in losses. A 12-year-old boy was charged with second-degree arson for starting the fires. (7/13/1982)

THE ICY FIRE AFTERMATH. Troy firemen walk past an ice-coated truck after battling a stubborn fire at the Collins Lumber Corporation in Troy. The fire destroyed three buildings and was difficult to fight because of the wind and cold temperatures. Collins rebuilt and remains in business today at the same location. (2/25/1988)

THE WATERFORD FLOOD. Ed Fronczek (left) and Dave Ball paddle a canoe along Third Street in Waterford after the Mohawk River overflowed. Ball's home is the white one in the background. The Mohawk River converges with the Hudson River nearby, which created trouble for Waterford residents, forcing 150 people to be evacuated. (1/20/1996)

THE TROY FLOOD, THE DAY AFTER. The flood left large chunks of ice covering the cars parked behind the Quayside Apartments along the Hudson River. The water receded quickly but caused considerable damage. (1/21/1996)

THE TROY FLOOD. Cars are under water behind the Quayside Apartments along River Street in Troy after the Hudson River overflowed its banks. Warm weather and heavy rains following heavy early snow created a situation in which both the Hudson and Mohawk Rivers flooded. (1/20/1996)

A TORNADO. Joseph Printy walks past the remains of his home on West Street in the town of Stillwater after a late-afternoon tornado ripped through the area, damaging many homes and leaving a path of destruction just west of the Hudson River. (5/31/1998)

TORNADO SURVIVORS. People walk down West Street in Stillwater after surviving a late-afternoon tornado, which devastated their neighborhood. Amazingly there were no fatalities associated with the tornado, which did extensive damage to this community. (5/31/1998)

ACT UP. Nearly 1,000 AIDS activists jammed traffic, blocked stairways, and shouted down Gov. Mario Cuomo in a daylong 1960s-style assault on the state capitol. They wrapped themselves in red tape to protest the amount of time it took to get help and staged "die-ins" on the street in front of the capitol. Demonstrations are common in Albany, but few have been as creative or passionate as the AIDS activists. (3/28/1990)

PROTESTOR ARRESTED. A state trooper drags a protestor through the glass doors that were smashed during a budget protest at the state capitol in Albany by state university students. The door leads to the executive chamber, where the governor's office is located. The students were protesting tuition hikes when a group of them became destructive. Security is much tighter at the capitol now, but the students return almost every year to protest any increase in tuition. (3/19/1991)

A CAGED ANIMAL. Kim Krier, painted to resemble a tiger and wearing only pasties and panties, squats in a cage on a busy corner in Albany to protest the treatment of wild animals by circuses. The protest, organized by People for the Ethical Treatment of Animals, took place the day Ringling Brothers, Barnum & Bailey Circus opened at the Pepsi Arena in Albany. PETA has used the same approach in other cities. (5/25/200)

GRAMPA LEWIS. Al "Grampa" Lewis, best known for his role on the television series *The Munsters,* joins others in protesting the Rockefeller Drug Laws, which require mandatory sentencing for drug-related arrests. Lewis ran for governor as the Green Party candidate but lost in his bid to use "Grampa" instead of his actual first name on the ballot. He was soundly defeated in the election as well. (3/3/1999)

DEPARTING SOLDIERS. Lee Hilt of West Sand Lake holds his son Liam as he receives instructions at the Albany County Airport. Hilt was one of 120 Marine reservists who were headed for Camp Lejeune in North Carolina before departing for Saudi Arabia. (11/27/1990)

CONDUCTOR CAREY. Gov. Hugh Carey gladly accepts the conductor's wand and leads the Albany Symphony Orchestra in a rendition of the Harvest of Music Festival's theme song, "I Love New York." The song's composer, Steve Karmen, lends a helping hand. The daylong festival took place at the Empire State Plaza in Albany. (10/11/1980)

MAKING A POINT. During a news conference in Albany, Gov. Hugh Carey climbed on his desk to dramatize his concern that lawmakers were being unrealistic in their budget proposal. In this unusual display, Carey remarked, "I measure 5 feet 10 inches tall. I can make believe I'm 10 feet tall, but I'm not and that's not the way I'm going to write a budget." (3/29/1980)

JESSE JACKSON. Democratic presidential candidate Jesse Jackson holds two children after delivering a campaign speech in the Empire State Plaza concourse near the state capitol. Jackson, a regular visitor to Albany, always draws enthusiastic crowds to hear his message. (4/14/1988)

HOWARD DEAN. Vermont governor Howard Dean waves to people as he marches in the annual Bennington Battle Day parade. Dean was making his first appearance as governor after Gov. Richard Snelling died suddenly of a heart attack. Dean, a practicing physician, was notified while treating a patient. Dean went on be reelected five times before becoming a candidate for the presidential nomination of the Democratic Party in 2004. (8/18/1991)

MICHAEL MCNULTY. U.S. representative Michael McNulty exults while holding his two-year-old granddaughter, Teigin McNulty, after defeating Lee Wasserman in a Democratic primary. McNulty, the former mayor of Green Island and state assemblyman, received one of his stiffest challenges in the primary. He went on to win reelection and is currently serving his eighth term in Congress. (9/10/1996)

JERRY JENNINGS. A jubilant Mayor Jerry Jennings greets a crowd of supporters at the Omni Hotel after winning a primary race against challenger Jack McEneny. Jennings won the general election easily and is currently serving his third term as mayor of Albany. (9/9/1997)

MARK PATTISON. Councilman Ed McGrath embraces Mark Pattison after Pattison's reelection as mayor of Troy. On the left is Councilman Dan Doran. For Pattison, it was very different from his first race for mayor, which was decided a week after the election on the basis of absentee ballots. (11/3/1999)

ROBERT SIGNORACCI. Cohoes mayor Robert Signoracci celebrates winning the city's Democratic mayoral primary race. Signoracci, who was seeking a second term, was challenged from within his party. He went on to win the general election. (9/12/1995)

DANIEL PATRICK MOYNIHAN. U.S. senator Daniel Patrick Moynihan makes a point during an editorial board meeting at the *Record* in Troy. A Democrat from New York, Moynihan served in the Senate for 24 years before retiring in 2000. A former U.S. ambassador to the United Nations, Moynihan was a popular vote-getter and highly respected leader of the Senate. He died three years after retirement. (12/12/1990)

ERASTUS CORNING. Albany mayor Erastus Corning II announces his plans to seek reelection during a news conference on the steps of city hall. Corning, who served as mayor for 42 years, was reelected in November 1981. He became ill and died in office in 1983. He was the longest-tenured mayor of any city in the United States. (6/18/1981)

JOHN SWEENEY. Lansingburgh native John Sweeney celebrates his election to Congress with supporters at the Holiday Inn in Saratoga Springs. He replaced longtime representative Jerry Solomon, who retired. It was Sweeney's first run for elected office. He has been reelected twice and is still serving in Congress. (11/3/1998)

SWEENEY AND SOLOMON. John Sweeney receives kind words from Jerry Solomon at a reception in Sweeney's office following Sweeney's swearing-in ceremony in the U.S. Capitol. Solomon served for 22 years as the congressman from the 22nd District, which spans nine counties and 240 miles in upstate New York. (1/6/1999)

BILL CLINTON. Pres. Bill Clinton shakes hands with Gov. Mario Cuomo after conducting a teleconference with the governor from the University at Albany campus. Clinton's trip was an attempt to assist Cuomo in his bid for a fourth term. The bid failed as Cuomo lost to George Pataki in the November election. (11/3/1994)

GEORGE H.W. BUSH. Vice Pres. George H.W. Bush greets a breakfast crowd during a campaign stop at the Ramada Inn in Schenectady. Bush, who was seeking the Republican presidential nomination, went on to become president after serving for eight years as vice president under Ronald Reagan. Bush served as president for one term. (4/12/1988)

AL GORE. Vice Pres. Al Gore addresses the Black and Puerto Rican Caucus in Wilborn Temple in Albany. Gore went on to earn the Democratic nomination for president but eventually lost one of the closest presidential elections in our nation's history to George W. Bush. (2/20/2003)

AL GORE AND HILLARY CLINTON. Vice Pres. Al Gore, who was running for the presidency, joins First Lady Hillary Rodham Clinton before each spoke at the Black and Puerto Rican Caucus service at the Wilborn Temple in Albany. This was the first time the two campaigned together after Clinton announced she was running for the U.S. Senate. She went on to win the election, becoming the first sitting First Lady in the nation's history to be elected to office. (2/20/2000)

GEORGE PATAKI ON TOUR. Joe Fama (left), executive director of the Troy Architectural Program, and state senate majority leader Joseph L. Bruno both point to different things Gov. George Pataki should notice as they take a walking tour of downtown Troy. (6/20/2000)

THE 175TH-ANNIVERSARY MASS. Bishop Howard Hubbard of the Roman Catholic Diocese of Albany offers communion during the 175th-anniversary mass at St. Peter's Church in Troy. On the left is Harry Flynn, archbishop of St. Paul-Minneapolis, and on the right is Rev. Thomas K. Flanigan, pastor of St. Peter's Church, the oldest Catholic church east of the Hudson River. (10/31/1999)

DAVID BALL. David Standish Ball of Menands is consecrated as bishop of the Episcopal Diocese of Albany during a three-hour ceremony at the Cathedral of All Saints in Albany. Ball assumed the role of bishop when the Rt. Rev. Wilbur E. Hogg retired. (2/20/1984)

THE PEACE PAGODA. People gather at the Peace Pagoda in Grafton to commemorate the 50th anniversary of the dropping of the atomic bomb on the Japanese city of Hiroshima during World War II. (8/16/1995)

A MOTHER AND DAUGHTER. Anne Ryan of Delmar, holding her five-month-old daughter, Willow, listens to remarks at the University at Albany after the college's unity walk. This event, like many others, was held in the aftermath of the terrorist attacks of September 11, 2001. Willow is an Old English name that means freedom. (9/12/2001)

JOHN RAMAHLO. John Ramahlo is sworn in as the lone Republican on the North Greenbush Town Board. Holding the Bible is his wife, Pamela, while his six-year-old son, Justin (the youngest of the three Ramahlo children), tries to watch. A year later, John Ramahlo was charged with killing his estranged wife. In a high-profile trial, Ramahlo, represented by defense attorney E. Stewart Jones, was convicted of manslaughter and sentenced to prison. Ramahlo was freed in 2003. (1/1/1991)

RAMAHLO LED AWAY. John Juris (left) and Jim Karam, deputy sheriffs, lead John Ramahlo away after a bail hearing in Rensselaer County Court. Ramahlo was later released on bail and he resumed his normal activities, including continuing in his elected office in North Greenbush until his trial. (1/13/1992)

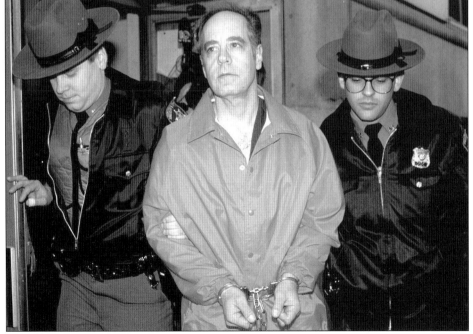

REV. AL SHARPTON. Rev. Al Sharpton gestures as he speaks with supporters of Amadou Diallo in Academy Park in front of the Albany County Courthouse. The door in the background has the silhouette of Diallo with the 19 bullets that struck him marked on it. The dots represent the 22 other shots, which missed him. Diallo was shot by four New York City police officers in a dark apartment hallway. Diallo, an immigrant, was reaching for his identification, and police thought he was going for a gun. The controversial trial for the officers was moved to Albany, where they were found not guilty. The shooting was labeled a tragic accident. (2/22/2003)

RAYMOND HENRY. Raymond C. Henry, Troy's honorary fire chief, stands in front of a plaque dedicating the Bouton Road Firehouse in his honor. Henry, an art teacher by profession, had been an honorary battalion chief since 1957. (10/20/1989)

THE SUNNYSIDE FIRE. Flames pour from a second-floor window at 7 West Sunnyside in Troy. Firefighters had a difficult time with the two-alarm fire, as two barking dogs greeted them and there was concern about exploding gunpowder from within the residence. No one was home at the time the fire broke out, and there were no injuries reported. (4/8/1992)

POSING FIREMEN. Members of the Latham Fire Department pose for a group photograph, seemingly oblivious to the building going up in flames behind them. Actually they had set fire to the abandoned building on New Loudon Road as part of a training drill. They extinguished the flames after the photograph was taken. (11/14/1987)

BILL O'REILLY. Bill O'Reilly, Fox News host of *The O'Reilly Factor,* listens as he is introduced as the distinguished speaker at the National Italian American Bar Association annual luncheon held at the Desmond Hotel in Colonie. O'Reilly, who has also authored three books, has been called one of the most influential people in television news today. (8/17/2001)

PATRICK BUCHANAN AND UNCLE SAM. Republican presidential candidate Patrick Buchanan shakes hands with Uncle Sam, portrayed by Fred Polnisch, at Mario's in Troy during a campaign stop. Troy is the home of Sam Wilson (Uncle Sam). (11/19/1995)

A WAVE FROM THE FIRST LADY. Hillary Rodham Clinton, flanked by Mayor Mark Pattison (left) and Assemblyman Ron Canestrari, waves to a crowd assembled outside Manory's Restaurant in Troy, where she stopped for a working lunch. Moments later, Clinton crossed the street and visited with the crowd and posed for photographs. (9/25/1999)

HILLARY RODHAM CLINTON. The First Lady greets children and poses for photographs on a visit to Troy. Clinton found out the children had just attended a photography class and were out to photograph the city. She departed from her plans briefly to greet them and give the children some closeups. (9/25/1999)

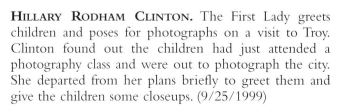

UNCLE SAM'S GRAVE SITE. Troy city councilman and veteran Marty Mahar salutes during the annual graveside ceremony remembering Uncle Sam Wilson, the meat packer from Troy who became a national icon. Wilson is buried in historic Oakwood Cemetery in Troy. (9/11/1993)

SEN. CHARLES SCHUMER. U.S. senator Charles Schumer bows his head in prayer after helping Samuel Prayer, first vice president of Albany's 369 Veteran's Association, place a wreath beneath the monument of Henry Johnson in Albany's Washington Park. Johnson, a black American, fought in World War I for France and was given its highest military recognition. (5/29/1999)

CHESTER A. ARTHUR. State assemblyman and war veteran Robert Prentiss delivers remarks during the annual tribute to Pres. Chester A. Arthur, the 21st president, who is buried in Albany Rural Cemetery. (5/28/1995)

Jacqueline Kennedy Onassis. Former First Lady Jacqueline Kennedy Onassis leaves one of the hearing rooms in the legislative office building next to the state capitol in Albany after testifying against legislation that would have exempted religious properties from local preservation laws. Onassis was a member of the committee trying to save St. Bartholomew's Church in New York City. (2/8/1984)

CHAPTER 2
FEATURES

THE OLYMPIC TORCHBEARER. Clara Hunt of Troy carries the Olympic torch on River Street. The torch stopped in Troy as it wound its way across America. (6/14/1996)

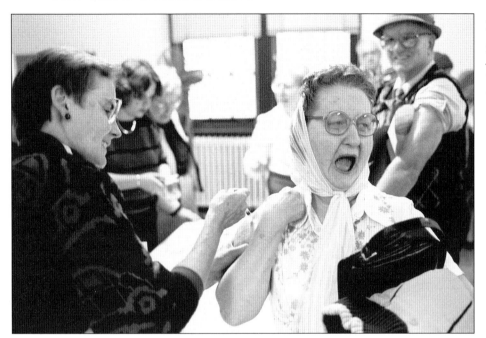

FLU SHOTS FOR SENIORS. Roseanne Van Vraken grimaces as she receives a flu shot from public health nurse Joan Muir at the Troy Senior Center. Anyone over the age of 60 could get the shot courtesy of the Rensselaer County Health Department. (10/28/1987)

IN THE DUNKING BOOTH. West Sand Lake Elementary School principal Dr. Larry Schrader heads for the water as he is dunked by students at his school. Schrader agreed to sit in the dunking booth if the student body read a certain number of books in a reading program. The students exceeded the number, and true to his word, Schrader spent the afternoon getting dunked. (6/20/1995)

AN ARCHER. John Vozzy of Waterford, a world-class archer, takes aim at a wild turkey during the early-morning hours. With sharp vision and a keen sense of smell turkeys are difficult prey. Vozzy claimed a silver medal at a world competition in Indonesia two months before this photograph was taken. (11/4/1995)

TROY'S BIRTHDAY. Students from Troy's three colleges—Russell Sage, Rensselaer Polytechnic Institute, and Hudson Valley Community College—present 200 cakes, one for each year since Troy's founding, to city officials in front of city hall. This was one of the many bicentennial festivities that took place during the year. (10/13/1989)

A WATERVLIET PARADE. Rep. Sam Stratton (center) joins Mayor J. Leo O'Brien as they applaud one of the marching bands during the city of Watervliet's 200th-anniversary parade. O'Brien was mayor of Watervliet for 23 years. (7/9/1988)

BRUNSWICK'S ANNIVERSARY. Harold Ives and Kenneth Clickner demonstrate how bartering was conducted to pay rent and purchase items 175 years ago as they ride on a float in the Brunswick anniversary parade. (6/5/1982)

A PETERSBURGH PARADE. A line of tractors proceeds along Route 22 in the rural Rensselaer County town of Petersburgh during a parade celebrating the town's 200th anniversary. (9/28/1991)

THE TRICENTENNIAL PARADE. The tricentennial parade proceeds down Washington Avenue, attracting an estimated 100,000 spectators to celebrate Albany's 300th anniversary. Albany is the capital of New York State. (7/19/1986)

A BALLOON LAUNCH. Balloons lift off from Albany's Lincoln Park with the Empire State Plaza in the background. The hot-air balloon launch was part of the tricentennial celebration. (7/22/1986)

BANKING IN THE SADDLE. Troy police officer Sam Carella uses the drive-through window at Trustco Bank in Troy while riding Fairclough. Riding the horse up to the bank window is a good training exercise, according to Carella. While Troy no longer has a mounted unit, Carella is able to borrow a horse from the New York State Parks Service and on occasion is still seen riding the streets of Troy. (8/24/1999)

A WEDDING ON THE COMET. Tim Church and Robin McCarthy exchange wedding vows at the top of the Comet roller coaster at the Great Escape and Splashwater Kingdom in Lake George. Schodack town justice Paul Peter performed the ceremony, the first wedding on the Comet. (8/20/1995)

A REVOLUTIONARY WEDDING. Wearing Revolutionary War–era attire, Ron Glasser and Kathy Rockenstire of Watervliet are married in a ceremony along the Mohawk River in the town of Colonie Park. William Hegeman officiated at the ceremony with the Mohawk River as a backdrop. (10/13/2001)

A WEDDING ON PARADE. Charlene McFarland and Gary Fredette are married atop a three-tiered wedding cake float by Troy mayor Robert Conway during the Uncle Sam parade. The float stopped near the bride's family home at 114th Street and Fifth Avenue, and the brief ceremony took place. (9/13/1992)

A KOREAN WAR VETERAN. Willie McDuffie of Albany, a Korean War veteran, wipes away a tear during a ceremony prior to the annual Veterans Day parade in Albany. (11/12/1990)

A VETERAN AND SON. Jay Cavey of Clifton Park, a Marine Corps veteran who served in Vietnam, attends a Veterans Day ceremony in Albany with his three-year-old son, Jay Walter Cavey. (11/11/1988)

TROY'S VIETNAM MEMORIAL. Veterans place a wreath next to the Vietnam memorial in Troy's Riverfront Park during a morning walk. They placed wreaths before three monuments downtown. The color guard is from the Marine Corps League, Troy Detachment. (11/11/1998)

THE FROG PROFESSOR. Prof. Bill Steed, dean of frogs and founder of Croaker College, encourages one of his frogs to lift weights during a presentation at the Record's downtown Troy office. Steed, who was in the area with his unique program, visited the Record office and showcased the talents of his bullfrogs. (1/7/1987)

TOTO. Toto the elephant, a member of the Big Apple Circus, performs in Troy's Barker Park to promote the circus that was in Troy for several performances. (7/1984)

THE 112TH STREET BRIDGE. This view of the new 112th Street Bridge looks north from Troy toward Cohoes just after sunset, with the lights reflecting on the icy Hudson River. (1/2/2001)

BLOWN UP. The 112th Street Bridge, which connects Cohoes on the west side of the Hudson River to Troy on the east, is demolished in a controlled explosion. Hundreds of bystanders gathered to watch the event, which paved the way for construction of a new bridge. (4/11/1996)

THE POLAR BEAR CLUB. Pablo Martinez Velia, a member of the Coney Island Polar Bear Club, rests under the ice during a swim in Lake George as part of the village's annual winter festival. The Coney Island Club no longer visits Lake George, but the locals have a Polar Bear Club, which goes in the frigid waters every New Year's Day. (2/14/1981)

A TUGBOAT. The tug *Stephen-Scott* pushes a barge laden with 24,000 barrels of fuel oil through the frozen Hudson River to make deliveries in the Capital District. The city of Troy and the Green Island Bridge are visible in the background. (1/12/2001)

ST. NICHOLAS. Paul Phillippsen portrays St. Nicholas as he walks around downtown Troy during the 10th annual Victorian Stroll, organized by the downtown merchants. (12/6/1992)

FATHER CHRISTMAS. Patrick Sisti of Indian Lake, portraying Father Christmas, kneels to visit with children during Troy's annual Victorian Stroll. (12/5/1999)

SLEEPING GRADUATES. Jennifer Brayman rests after the fruits of her academic labor came to a close during graduation ceremonies for the Unity Sunshine Program in Troy. Classmate Billy White seems ready to follow suit while Vernon Dane watches the sleepy scholars in awe. (6/25/1987)

MASKED GRADUATES. Rensselaer Polytechnic Institute's architectural students hold handmade white masks in keeping with the architectural tradition of wearing nontraditional commencement garb. (5/15/1987)

SHIRLEY ANN JACKSON AND BILL COSBY. Rensselaer Polytechnic Institute president Dr. Shirley Ann Jackson gets a hug from entertainer Bill Cosby after he delivered the address at the college's 195th commencement at Albany's Pepsi Arena. Cosby removed his cap and gown and delivered the address in a Rensselaer sweatshirt. (5/12/2001)

RPI PENCIL GRADUATES. Keeping alive a Rensselaer Polytechnic Institute tradition, the architecture school graduates designed No. 2 pencils for their caps in sharp contrast to the traditionally garbed M. Jeffrey Baker in the foreground. For many years the architecture graduates as a group came up with unique attire for commencement. They no longer do this as a group. (5/16/1986)

SERVING BREAKFAST. George Low, the 14th president of Rensselaer Polytechnic Institute, serves breakfast to students who had spent weeks waiting outside the student union for hockey tickets to go on sale. In order to get good seats, students, usually in groups, would rotate in the "hockey line" sometimes sleeping there, while waiting for tickets to go on sale. Low, in keeping with the tradition that recently ended, served breakfast the morning of the sale. (10/8/1979)

A SENATOR AT RPI. U.S. senator Daniel Patrick Moynihan (left) marches with Rensselaer Polytechnic Institute president George Low on commencement day at the Troy college. Rensselaer is the oldest school of technology in the country. Moynihan received an honorary degree and delivered the commencement address at the school's 177th commencement. (5/20/1983)

THE UNCLE SAM CHORUS. The Uncle Sam Chorus, with Fred Polnisch portraying Uncle Sam, sings during the annual Uncle Sam parade in Lansingburgh. The parade is held on a Sunday close to the birth date of Sam Wilson, who became known as Uncle Sam. (9/15/1996)

MIRINDA JAMES. Local singer Mirinda James performs in Knickerbacker Park after the Uncle Sam parade. James, from Scotia, appeared in the parade and performed in the festivities that followed. James, considered a child prodigy, continues to sing and now resides in Los Angeles. (9/12/1993)

THE LA SALLE BAND. The La Salle Institute Band marches in the annual Flag Day parade through downtown Troy. (6/14/2000)

A FLAG DAY PARADE. The St. Peter-St. Patrick's Band passes beneath the giant flag that flies above Fourth Street in Troy during the 32nd annual Flag Day parade, which is believed to be the largest Flag Day parade in America. (6/13/1999)

A WING WALKER. Teresa Stokes performs on the wing of a biplane flown by Gene Soucy as part of the airshow at Schenectady County Airport. Stokes has performed for many years with Soucy, and they are regulars at airshows across the country. (9/6/1996)

PROPHET FOSTER. Prophet Foster pushes up his mask after pouring bronze at Wheeler Brothers Brass Foundry in Troy. The business, which started around the turn of century, specialized in custom castings that ranged from parts for NASA moon vehicles to bronze figures for artists. Wheeler Brothers, which is now closed, gained notoriety for casting horseshoes for Pres. George H. W. Bush. (11/26/1986)

LT. GOV. MARY DONOHUE. Lt. Gov. Mary Donohue answers questions while visiting fifth-graders at School 18 in Troy to discuss character education. Donohue spoke in the same room in which she once taught before she returned to law school. The Troy native was elected Rensselaer County district attorney and state supreme court judge before becoming lieutenant governor with Gov. George Pataki. (5/9/2002)

SEN. JOSEPH L. BRUNO. State senator Joseph L. Bruno, dressed in Western garb, rides his horse Apache during the Memorial Day parade in Rensselaer. A year and half later, the Republican from Brunswick was elected to head the state senate and became senate majority leader. He continues in this position today. (5/30/1993)

CORETTA SCOTT KING. Rev. Hugh F. Hines, president of Siena College in Loudonville, leads the applause for Coretta Scott King, widow of slain civil rights leader Dr. Martin Luther King Jr. She visited the college to receive an honorary degree for advocating peaceful resistance to social ills. (4/16/1986)

BACKFLIPPING. Children calling themselves the Troy Tigers teach themselves how to do backflips using an abandoned mattress in a field south of the Collar City Bridge. (9/9/1996)

YO-YOING. Needing a little additional height, four-year-old Philip Baker, with the help of his father, Scott Baker, uses a mailbox to learn the art of working a yo-yo. The activity was part of an old-fashioned games program at the Troy Public Library. (7/17/1985)

THE BATTLE OF SARATOGA. The British troops fire at the patriots during the 225th anniversary of the Battle of Saratoga reenactment, held on a farm in Fort Edward. The redcoats won this battle but lost the next day in one of the important Revolutionary War battles. The event drew more than 3,000 reenactors, who were forced to use private land since the actual site, a federal park, prohibits people from firing guns at each other. To the right, the Colonial army advances. On day two of the reenactment, the patriots were victorious and the battles helped turn the tide in the Revolutionary War. (10/12/2002)

A GOLFING NUN. Sister Mary, of St. Colman's Home in Watervliet, works on her swing on the driving range at Western Turnpike Golf Course in Guilderland before teeing off in the fourth annual St. Colman's Golf Tournament, a fundraising event. She went on to win one of the longest drive contests at the tournament. (6/28/2000)

CHAPTER 3
SPORTS

LEAPING FOR JOY. Siena College's Brian Bidlingmyer leaps for joy as his team defeats Georgia Tech in a National Invitational Tournament game at Albany's Knickerbacker Arena (now known as the Pepsi Arena). The game drew a capacity crowd and was considered one of the college's most important wins. (3/21/1994)

SCOTTISH GOLF. Lou Schenck of East Berne putts on the second hole in the morning fog during the Scottish Games' second annual charity golf tournament at Stadium Golf Club in Schenectady. The games take place each year at the Altamont Fairgrounds on Labor Day weekend. The golf tournament is played earlier in the year and attracts some golfers in their kilts. (8/17/1998)

A MUDDY SLIDE. Greenwich High School soccer players Miranda Curley (left), Erin Barmhart (center), and Nikki Gerardi dive through the mud in front of one of the goals after a heavy downpour postponed their scheduled home game against Tamarac. (10/14/1998)

DOTTIE PEPPER MOCHRIE. Dottie Pepper Mochrie of Saratoga Springs putts during play on the Ladies Professional Golf Association tour event in Stratton, Vermont. Mochrie, who still competes on the tour, has won 15 LPGA events and was player of the year in 1992. (8/6/1992)

A BIRDIE ON THE 18TH. Mike Callahan pumps his fist after sinking a birdie putt on the 18th hole, forcing a playoff in the Rensselaer County Amateur tournament at Troy's Frear Park. Callahan went on to win his second consecutive title. He has won the event on two more occasions. (9/11/1994)

LEE TREVINO. Well-known golfer Lee Trevino gestures to the crowd while conducting a clinic prior to the fifth annual Capital Skins Game at Shaker Ridge Country Club in Colonie. The fundraising event benefits Ellis Hospital in Schenectady. (6/17/1997)

ARNOLD PALMER. Golfing legend Arnold Palmer watches the first ball ever hit with a driver he built in his home golf shop. Palmer played in the 10th annual Skins Game at Mohawk Country Club in Schenectady. It was the second time Palmer played in the event. (6/25/2002)

MIKE TYSON. Mike Tyson (right) listens while his mentor and trainer, Cus D'Amato, talks during a news conference announcing a professional boxing card and the professional debut of Tyson at the Empire State Plaza Convention Center. It was at this event in Albany that D'Amato predicted Tyson would become the youngest heavyweight champion in history. D'Amato was correct, as Tyson did become the youngest champion. (2/19/1985)

TYSON VERSUS TILLIS. Mike Tyson (right) battles James "Quick" Tillis in a heavyweight bout at the Glens Falls Civic Center. Tillis, who lost a unanimous decision, was the first fighter to go the distance with Tyson. The victory improved Tyson's record to 20-0 and helped him eventually become the youngest heavyweight champion in history. (5/3/1986)

A TYSON PORTRAIT. A determined Mike Tyson takes a break from training at St. Joseph's Youth Center in Albany in preparation for a heavyweight bout with Razor Ruddock. Tyson held a workout open to area youth. During his early career, Tyson trained in the town of Catskill and fought most of his fights in the Albany area. (10/7/1989)

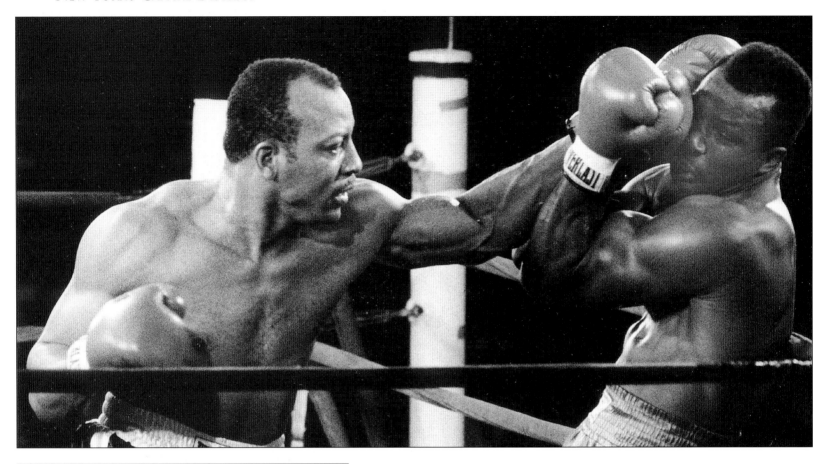

BONECRUSHER SMITH. James "Bonecrusher" Smith lands a hard left to Mike Weaver's face in their heavyweight fight at the Starlight Theater in Latham. Smith knocked out Weaver at 2:29 of the first round. (4/5/1986)

POMPEY VERSUS SMITH. Kevin Pompey (right) of Troy battles Buck Smith in a U.S. Boxing Association welterweight title fight in the Knickerbacker Recreational Facility in Lansingburgh. Pompey won a 12-round decision in the fight televised by ESPN. The beaten Buck Smith left Troy with a record of 124-3-1, the most wins in the country. (11/18/1992)

TACKLED IN THE SNOW. Lansingburgh's Kareem Jones is tackled by a Peru defender during the state quarterfinal game played in the snow at Colonie Central High School. Lansingburgh defeated the defending state champions, ending their 23-game winning streak. Jones, a junior, went on to set the all-time Section II rushing record his senior year. (11/16/2002)

AN UNBEATEN SEASON. Shenendehowa head coach Brent Steuerwald (left) and line coach Gene Stefanacci ride on the shoulders of their players after defeating Amsterdam, the defending champion, to finish an unbeaten season and win the Section II football championship 34–7. The game was played at Mount Pleasant High School in Schenectady. Steuerwald just finished his 36th season as head coach at Shenendehowa, where he has won 265 games—the most in Section II history and fifth most in New York State history. (11/14/1987)

A RECORD-SETTING SEASON. Shenendehowa's Lee Bates is tackled by Webster's Eddie Paffendorf during the New York State Class AA state championship game in the Carrier Dome at Syracuse University. Bates had a record-setting season in leading Shenendehowa to its first trip to the Carrier Dome. Webster won the game, leaving Shenendehowa with its only loss of the year. (12/1/2002)

STATE CHAMPIONS. Troy High School players celebrate after their win in the Class AA championship game at the Carrier Dome in Syracuse. Troy defeated Fairport, avenging a loss in the same game a year earlier. Troy High School, under coach Jack Burger, reached the state final four consecutive years, winning two titles. (11/29/1998)

THE FIREBIRDS' FINAL TOUCHDOWN. Albany fullback Jon Krick (left) and Leroy Thompson celebrate after scoring the Firebirds' final touchdown in the closing seconds against Orlando. The touchdown clinched Albany's first Arena Bowl victory in the franchise's 10-year history. The Firebirds relocated to Indianapolis after the 2000 season. (8/21/1999)

ANOTHER TOUCHDOWN. "Touchdown Eddie" Brown scores during an Albany Firebird game in Albany's Pepsi Arena. Brown earned his nickname by scoring frequently, including eight touchdowns in one game. He has led the league in scoring six times. In 1996, he became the first player in league history with more than 3,000 all-purpose yards in a single season. (5/4/1996)

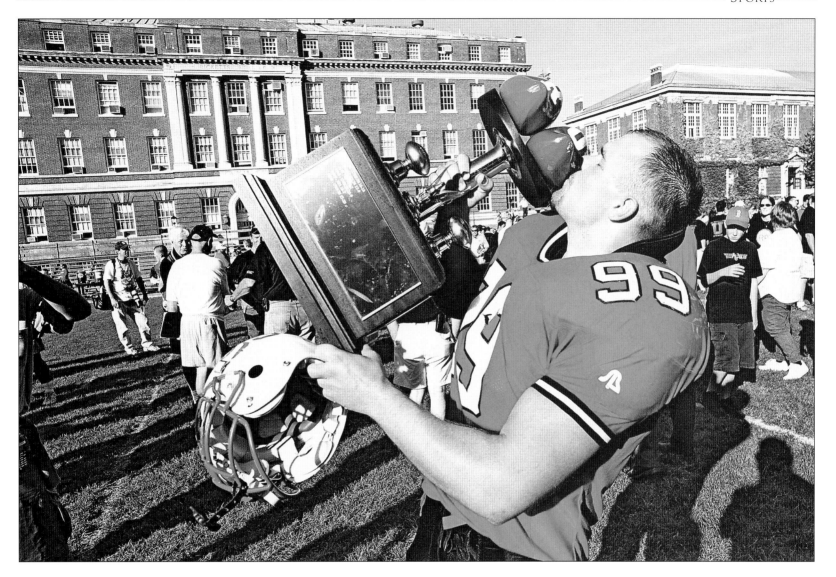

THE DUTCHMAN SHOES TROPHY. Rensselaer Polytechnic Institute's Ed Petkovsek, a senior captain, gives the Dutchman Shoes trophy a big kiss after Rensselaer defeated Union College in a battle of unbeatens. The annual Division III game is the oldest college football rivalry in New York State. In 2002, the two schools played for the 100th time. (10/13/2001)

JEREMY SHOCKEY. New York Giants tight end Jeremy Shockey encourages his teammates during training camp in Albany. Shockey, a rookie in 2002, quickly became an outspoken team leader and is regarded as one of the National Football League's premier tight ends. (8/5/2003)

KERRY COLLINS. New York Giants quarterback Kerry Collins practices with a medicine ball during an afternoon practice at the Giants training camp on the grounds at the University at Albany. (8/8/2002)

ANDRE AGASSI. At age 16, Andre Agassi, the surprise of the tournament, leaves the court after winning a semifinal match in the OTB Tennis Open in Schenectady. Agassi lost the final, but his performance here was an indication of what was to come. He has gone on to win all four Grand Slam events and has been the No. 1–ranked player in the world during a career that has established him as one of the all-time great American players. (7/19/1986)

PETE SAMPRAS. Pete Sampras, age 16, returns a shot during a semifinal match against Tim Mayotte in the OTB Tennis Open in Schenectady. Sampras lost the match, much as Agassi had two years earlier. Sampras also went on to become the top player in the world, retiring in 2003 with 14 Grand Slam titles, the most in the history of men's tennis. (7/23/1988)

BERNIE WILLIAMS. Bernie Williams loosens up in the on-deck circle during a season with the Albany-Colonie Yankees, the AA affiliate of the New York Yankees. Williams helped the team to a 70-22 record during the first part of the season. Williams has gone on to start in center field for the Yankees, appearing in five All-Star games and setting a record for the most postseason home runs in baseball history. (7/21/1989)

RON GUIDRY. New York Yankees pitching ace Ron Guidry warms up before pitching three innings for the Albany-Colonie Yankees in a rehabilitation start at Heritage Park. Guidry was recovering from a hand injury. The crowd of 14,491 was so large that some fans were allowed onto the field. These people were seated on the warning track against the fence in the outfield. (7/23/1986)

WATERVLIET CHAMPS. Watervliet catcher Yorden Huban (left) and tournament MVP Bob Hotaling celebrate with their teammates after winning the Class C state title in Utica. The state title was the third of the year for Watervliet, which had earlier won both the football and basketball titles. No school in the state has ever won all three in the same school year. (6/8/1991)

A DOUBLE PLAY. Watervliet shortstop Dominic Fruscio fires to first to complete a double play against Norwood–Norfolk during the state title game. Fruscio was one of three players to play on all three championship teams. The other two players were Yorden Huban and Billy Williams. (6/8/1991)

RUNNING WITH THE PACK. Tim O'Brien, running in full army gear including the 45-pound pack, gestures as he nears the finish line in the 10k race during Troy's 38th annual Thanksgiving morning Turkey Trot. O'Brien of Poestenkill, running for the 12th year, always carries the American flag. The race was held two months after the terrorist attacks of September 11, 2001, and O'Brien's patriotic display was warmly received by the crowd. (11/22/2001)

THE START OF THE TROT. Runners in the 5k division of the Thanksgiving morning Turkey Trot in Troy start on River Street in front of city hall and head east. The race features a 5k, 10k, and one-mile fun run, which collectively has attracted more than 3,000 runners in recent years. It has become a Thanksgiving morning tradition. (11/23/1995)

LYNN JENNINGS. Lynn Jennings of Newmarket, New Hampshire, enjoys the cooling spray of a fire hose after winning the 10th annual Freihofer's Run for Women. It was the second year in a row Jennings won the 10k race designated the TAC/USA women's championship. The championship is now the 5k race, and Jennings has won a total of five times, including holding the 5k record for this race. (5/28/1988)

A RIDERLESS HORSE. Richard McWade (No. 6) looks back at a riderless horse, Pine Hollow, during a steeplechase race at Saratoga Race Course. The horse dumped jockey Jeff Teter, who was not injured, and kept on running. (8/15/1986)

THE KING OF SARATOGA. Angel Cordero Jr. leaves the paddock at the Saratoga Race Course for another race. Cordero, dubbed "the King of Saratoga," won 11 straight riding titles at the Saratoga meet and 13 out of 14 from 1976 to 1989. (8/20/1980)

POINT GIVEN'S LAST RACE. Point Given, ridden by Gary Stevens, wins the 132nd running of the Travers Stakes Race at the Saratoga Race Course before some 60,000 spectators. The three-year-old thoroughbred had won the Preakness and Belmont Stakes earlier in the year and was named horse of the year. This was Point Given's final race, as he was retired just a week later after suffering a leg injury. (8/25/2001)

NAMED COACH. Louis Orr weeps openly after being named Siena College men's basketball coach. After composing himself, Orr admitted he is an emotional person who cries at church and at movies. Orr coached at Siena for only one season before moving on to coach at Seton Hall in the Big East conference. (4/24/2000)

LOUIS ORR GUARDING MICHAEL JORDAN. Playing for the New York Knicks, Louis Orr defends rookie guard Michael Jordan of the Chicago Bulls during a preseason game at a sold-out Glens Falls Civic Center. It was Jordan's fifth game as a professional, and he went on to help the Bulls win six National Basketball Association titles while earning the reputation as the game's all-time greatest player. (10/15/1984)

SAM PERKINS. Sam Perkins shoots over Troy High School defender James Mayben during the Section II Class A semifinal game at the Glens Falls Civic Center. Perkins scored 27 points to lead Shaker High School to an easy 72-40 victory. Christian Brothers Academy stunned Perkins and his unbeaten Shaker team in their next game, the sectional final. Perkins went on to star at North Carolina, playing with Michael Jordan and winning college basketball's national championship. He enjoyed a lengthy professional career before retiring after the 2002 season. (3/8/1980)

AN ACADEMY UPSET. A jubilant Bill Telasky, Christian Brothers Academy head coach, celebrates after his team upset the heavily favored and previously unbeaten Shaker High School, led by Sam Perkins, to win the Section II Class A title at the Glens Falls Civic Center. (3/12/1980)

PHIL JACKSON. Phil Jackson, on the court of the Washington Avenue Armory in Albany, coached the Albany Patroons for five seasons, winning one title in the now extinct Continental Basketball Association. He was named coach of the year once. Jackson has gone on to coach the Chicago Bulls and Los Angeles Lakers to nine NBA championships while winning more postseason games than any coach in NBA league history. (11/1985)

PAT RILEY. Los Angeles Lakers head coach Pat Riley, a native of Schenectady, takes some warmup shots before the ceremony dedicating the basketball courts in Schenectady's Central Park in his name. Riley, who retired from coaching to become president of the NBA Miami Heat in 2003, coached the Los Angeles Lakers to four titles and is the second winningest coach in NBA history. (8/13/1988)

CARMELLO ANTHONY. Syracuse freshman forward Carmello Anthony smiles as the clock runs out on Oklahoma during the National Collegiate Athletic Association Basketball East Regional Championship at the Pepsi Arena in Albany. Syracuse defeated Oklahoma to advance to the Final Four in New Orleans. (3/30/2003)

GERRY MCNAMARA. Syracuse freshman guard Gerry McNamara shoots against Oklahoma during play in the NCAA Basketball East Regional Championship at the Pepsi Arena in Albany. McNamara, along with teammate Carmello Anthony, helped lead Syracuse to its first national collegiate basketball championship. (3/30/2003)

SHENENDEHOWA SOCCER. Shenendehowa High School's Joel Andruski strikes the ball on goal in front of his teammate Peter Essele during their state quarterfinal tournament game against Fayetteville-Manlius at Colonie High School. (11/13/1999)

MIA HAMM. Mia Hamm, a member of the U.S. national women's team, hugs Luke Noll (left) and Dillon Campbell, both nine-year-old third-graders, during a game Hamm played with the students at the Dorothy Nolan Elementary School in Saratoga Springs. Hamm was in town to hold a private clinic at the school. (6/5/2001)

DOC SAUERS. Richard "Doc" Sauers watches as his University at Albany Great Danes defeat Montclair State for his 600th career victory. Sauers, who retired in 1997 with a record of 702-330, had only one losing season in the 41 years he coached at the University at Albany. Sauers is in the school's hall of fame. (1/4/1992)

MIKE ADDESA. Rensselaer Polytechnic Institute hockey coach Mike Addesa gives directions to his team during a home game. Addesa coached the team to the national championship during the 1984–1985 season but struggled the following year. He left the Troy university with 186 wins, the most by any hockey coach in the school's history. (3/17/1986)

A TROY LOSS. Troy High School starters Maureen Holohan (left), Marcell Harrison (center), and Nikki Hilton show their emotions after losing the Section II title game to rival Shenendehowa. Troy had defeated Shenendehowa the previous year but could not defend the title. The intense rivalry between the two schools helped elevate girls' basketball to a high level in the Capital District. (3/3/1990)

DIVING FOR THE BALL. Catholic Central High School's Chris Spain, along with teammates Josh Gibbs (far left) and Jason Bariteau, tries to corral the ball as Colonie High School's Mike Stevens gives chase. The wild sequence in the waning seconds of the game led to a Catholic Central High School foul on Colonie's Brian Larrabee. Larrabee made what proved to be the game-winning free throws as Colonie won 47-45 in the Class A semifinal sectional game played at the Glens Falls Civic Center. (3/7/1998)

TROY'S 1882-STYLE UNIFORMS. Members of the Troy baseball team, which played a team from Worcester, Massachusetts, model their 1882-style uniforms. Both Troy and Worcester were original members of the National League. They were voted out of the league and granted lifetime honorary membership in 1885. When voted out of the league, the series between the two teams was tied. Playing without gloves and by the rules of 1882, the two cities held a two-game series 110 years later to break the tie. Each team won on its home field, and to this day the series remains tied. (6/4/1992)

OUT AT FIRST. Tri-City Valley Cats second baseman Edwin Maysonet throws to first ahead of the sliding Mike Russell, completing a double play against Aberdeen during New York Penn Class A action at Joseph L. Bruno Stadium in Troy. Baseball returned to Troy with the construction of "the Joe" on the campus of Hudson Valley Community College in 2002. (7/7/2003)

CHAPTER 4
ARTS AND ENTERTAINMENT

TINA TURNER. Tina Turner performs at a sold-out Pepsi Arena in Albany on her farewell tour. Singer Joe Cocker performed before Turner took the stage. (9/23/2000)

A STAGED STRIKE. For this scene in the film *Ironweed*, an Albany street was transformed into a 1901 setting in which the action from a violent trolley strike was depicted. *Ironweed*, directed by Hector Babenco and starring Jack Nicholson and Meryl Streep, was filmed entirely in the Capital District. (5/30/1987)

WILLIAM KENNEDY. Pulitzer Prize–winning writer William Kennedy waits outside the Troy Public Library, where a scene from *Ironweed* was being filmed. Kennedy, of nearby Averill Park, wrote both the book and screenplay for the film based in Albany. (3/19/1987)

JACK NICHOLSON. Jack Nicholson, portraying Francis Phelan, works for a junk man in this scene from *Ironweed,* filmed in Troy's Washington Park. The film, based on the Pulitzer Prize–winning novel by William Kennedy, tells the story of Phelan's return to his home (Albany) after a 22-year exile. (3/25/1987)

A SEQUENCE FILMED AT EMMA WILLARD. Actor James Rebhorn, playing Mr. Trask, the headmaster, is the victim of a prank that leaves both him and his car covered in white paint in this scene from *Scent of a Woman*. Part of the film, directed by Martin Brest and starring Al Pacino and Chris O'Donnell, was filmed at the Emma Willard School in Troy. The school, an all-girls school, is depicted in the movie as an all-boys school. (12/11/1991)

KEVIN KLINE. Embeth Davidtz and Kevin Kline take a break from filming a scene in the *The Emperor's Club* on the Emma Willard campus in Troy. Kline, the film's star, portrays a respected teacher at a prestigious all-boys preparatory school. The all-girls Emma Willard School is once again transformed into an all-boys school for movie purposes. (5/7/2001)

YO-YO MA. Noted cellist Yo-Yo Ma speaks with the crowd gathered outside the Troy Savings Bank Music Hall for a free noontime performance. He was in Troy recording with Emmanuel Ax, Isaac Stern, and Jamie Laredo. The four renowned artists agreed to play a concert for the public after shunning publicity at a previous recording session. The crowd grew so large they changed plans and performed two concerts, both to capacity crowds of 1,250. The Troy Savings Bank Music Hall, which sits atop the downtown bank, is widely known for having extraordinary acoustics that attract top musicians to perform and record. (1/11/1990)

BENNY GOODMAN. The legendary Benny Goodman plays at the Troy Savings Bank Music Hall. (11/10/1979)

MITCH MILLER. Noted conductor Mitch Miller takes a moment to rehearse prior to his concert with the Albany Symphony Orchestra at the Troy Savings Bank Music Hall. Troy firefighter John Tilton kept a close eye on Miller and his cigar since the historic hall has a no-smoking policy. (4/20/1979)

THEDA BARA. Heritage Artists actors rehearse a scene from the production *Theda Bara and the Frontier Rabbi,* which premiered at the Cohoes Music Hall. Heritage Artists was the resident company at the historic theater in the late 1980s before departing due to financial struggles. The Cohoes Music Hall now has a new company, which began in 2002. (1/17/1989)

SLY FOX. Doug de Lisle and Jennifer Volpe rehearse a scene from *Sly Fox* at the Albany Civic Theater. The theater, which celebrated its 50th anniversary in 2003, produces four plays annually, using local talent. Doug de Lisle has appeared in or directed some two dozen productions. (9/18/1995)

RUBY DEE. Ruby Dee (left) embraces her friend and fellow actress Maureen Stapleton, who surprised her at a reception at Siena College. Dee was to deliver the annual Martin Luther King lecture the next day at the Loudonville college. Stapleton, from nearby Troy, arrived at the reception unexpectedly. (1/14/1991)

STARS OF *THE COTTON CLUB*. Gregory Hines (left), James Remar (center), and Vincent Jerosa, stars of the film, which premiered in Albany's Palace Theater, enjoy a drink at the reception after the screening. Local Pulitzer Prize–winning author William Kennedy cowrote the movie's screenplay with Francis Ford Coppola and Mario Puzo, which led to the East Coast premiere being held in Albany. (12/2/1984)

PHIL COLLINS. Pop star Phil Collins parades around a circular stage at the Pepsi Arena during his concert. Collins performed for more than two hours. (3/25/1997)

CHER. Cher performs at Albany's Pepsi Arena before a sold-out crowd. Cher returned in August 2003 during her farewell tour and once again performed before a sellout crowd. (7/16/1999)

JANET JACKSON. Janet Jackson performs at Albany's Pepsi Arena. The high-energy show with plenty of pyrotechnics wowed the crowd. Jackson had originally been scheduled to play on New Year's Eve but made up for the postponed show with a night to remember. (1/24/1994)

BRITNEY SPEARS. Britney Spears performs in Albany's Pepsi Arena the day after turning 20 years old. She appeared on the David Letterman show earlier the same night. It was Spears's second appearance at the Pepsi Arena. (12/3/2001)

ERNIE WILLIAMS. Ernie Williams performs at the Fleet Blues Festival at the Empire State Plaza in Albany. The event, like all held at the Empire State Plaza, was free and open to the public. Williams, who had been playing for more than 40 years, and his band, the Wildcats, became popular after Williams turned 70. Williams, now 78, continues to perform with his band, the Ernie Williams Band, throughout the Northeast. (7/10/1999)

TOMMY CASTRO. Tommy Castro, a San Francisco–based blues-rock star, performs in Troy's Riverfront Park during the Riverfront Arts Festival. Castro appeared for two consecutive years at the event while he was touring the East Coast. (6/15/1996)

BO DIDDLEY. Bo Diddley entertains a large crowd at the Empire State Plaza as the headline act in the annual Fleet Blues Festival. Bothered by a bad back, he sat for much of the show but warned the audience, "I'm just as dangerous sitting down." (7/12/2003)

JON BON JOVI. Jon Bon Jovi plays for a small select audience during a promotional tour at radio station FLY 92 in Colonie. Bon Jovi and three longtime members of his band, Richie Sambora, Tico Torres, and David Bryan, played several songs from their new album *Bounce*. (10/15/2002)

JACK KLUGMAN AND HUGH CAREY. Gov. Hugh Carey (right) talks to actor Jack Klugman in the winner's circle at the Saratoga Race Course after Klugman's horse, Jacklin Klugman, won a race. (8/16/1980)

KIRK DOUGLAS. Actor Kirk Douglas, originally from Amsterdam, stands on the press box roof at the historic Saratoga Race Course. Douglas, the guest of socialite Mary Lou Whitney, visited the track for the day. Douglas acknowledged the crowd and visited the roof to pose for photographers. (8/4/1984)

THE AGE OF INNOCENCE. The street in front of the Rice Building in downtown Troy is transformed into an 1870s New York City street for this scene from the film *The Age of Innocence.* The film, directed by Martin Scorcese and starring Daniel Day-Lewis, Michelle Pfeiffer, and Winona Ryder, was filmed in part in the Capital District. Based on an adaptation of Edith Wharton's novel, on morals and manners in New York society in the 1870s, the film was released one year after this scene was shot. (3/30/1992)

THE LAKEHOUSE ALIT. Albany's Washington Park lakehouse is illuminated for the holiday season as part of the Capital Lights in the Park month-long event. The public may tour the park and see different light displays for a charitable contribution to the Albany Police Athletic League. (11/22/1999)

THE TIME MACHINE. Dreamworks Productions films *The Time Machine* on Lancaster Street in Albany, with Mother Nature providing real snow. The street was transformed into a London street scene from *c.* 1899. The early part of the movie was filmed in Albany, Schenectady, and Troy. (2/8/2001)